It's a Big Country!

Written by Claire Owen

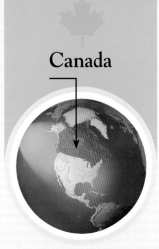

Canada

My name is Martine. I live in Québec, Canada. Look at a map of the world. Which country do you think is the largest? If the countries were listed in order of size, where do you think Canada would rank?

Contents

Wherever you see me, you'll find activities to try and questions to answer.

A Big Country

Canada is the second largest country in the world. It has an area of 3.85 million square miles. Canada's natural wonders include tall mountains, long rivers, and some of the world's largest lakes and islands. Canada also has the longest coastline in the world, measuring 151,485 miles. That is about six times the distance around the equator!

How much bigger than Canada is Russia? Pick two other countries from the chart on the next page. What is the difference in area?

World's Biggest Countries

Country	Area (Millions of Square Miles)
Russia	6.59
Canada	3.85
United States	3.72
China	3.71
Brazil	3.29
Australia	2.97
India	1.27
Argentina	1.07
Kazakhstan	1.05
Sudan	0.97

Niagara Falls from the Canadian side

Large Lakes

Canada has about two million lakes, covering almost one-twelfth of the country. Lake Superior, which spans the border between Canada and the United States, is the second largest lake in the world. Great Bear Lake is the largest lake entirely inside Canada. The lake is 1,356 feet deep. Great Bear Lake is frozen for at least two-thirds of the year.

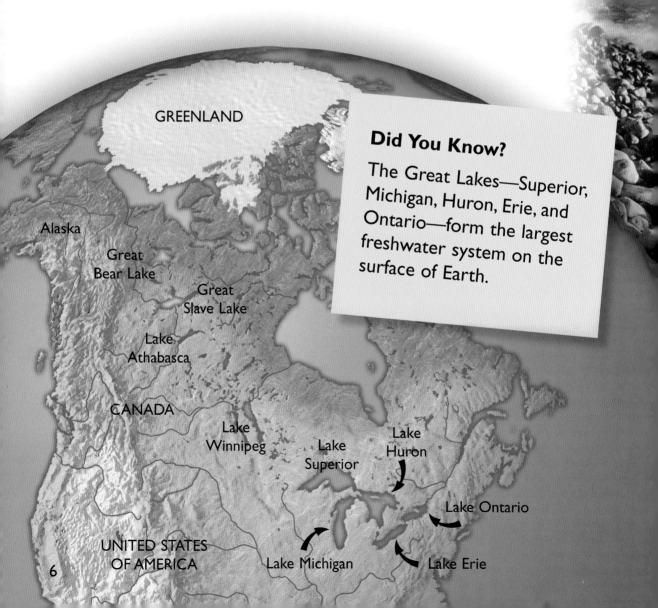

GREENLAND

Did You Know?

The Great Lakes—Superior, Michigan, Huron, Erie, and Ontario—form the largest freshwater system on the surface of Earth.

Alaska

Great Bear Lake

Great Slave Lake

Lake Athabasca

CANADA

Lake Winnipeg

Lake Superior

Lake Huron

Lake Ontario

UNITED STATES OF AMERICA

Lake Michigan

Lake Erie

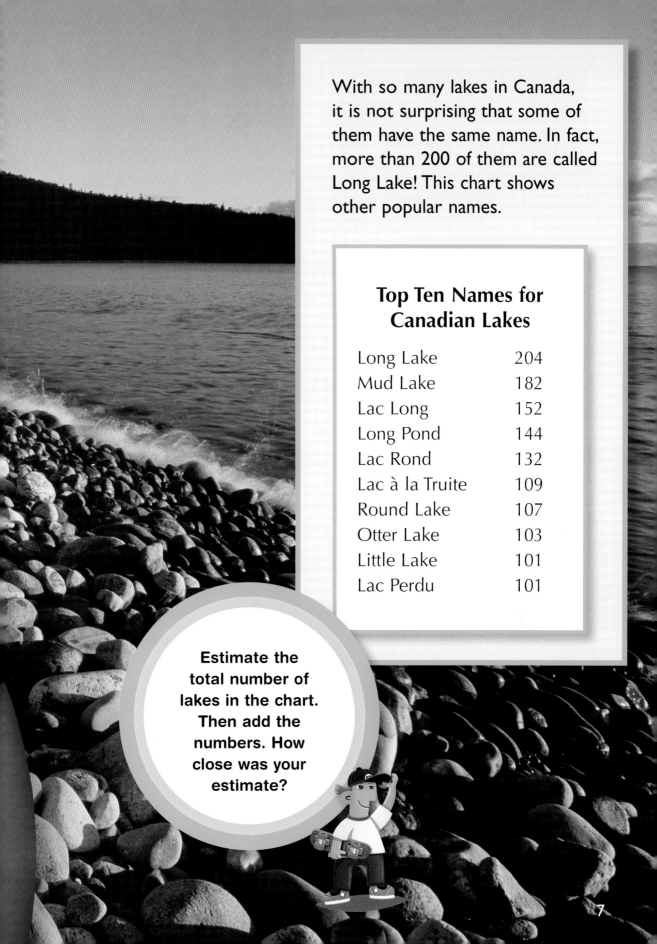

With so many lakes in Canada, it is not surprising that some of them have the same name. In fact, more than 200 of them are called Long Lake! This chart shows other popular names.

Top Ten Names for Canadian Lakes

Long Lake	204
Mud Lake	182
Lac Long	152
Long Pond	144
Lac Rond	132
Lac à la Truite	109
Round Lake	107
Otter Lake	103
Little Lake	101
Lac Perdu	101

Estimate the total number of lakes in the chart. Then add the numbers. How close was your estimate?

All the Rivers Run

Canada has many long rivers. Perhaps the most important is the St. Lawrence River. Together with the Great Lakes, the St. Lawrence provides 9,500 miles of waterways for shipping. A system of lakes, rivers, deepened channels, locks, and canals allows ships to sail from the Atlantic Ocean to the rich industrial and agricultural regions around the Great Lakes.

lock   part of a canal or river, with gates at either end, for lowering or raising vessels from one level to another

Canada's rivers are also used for sports such as kayaking and canoeing.

Which Canadian river is closest to 1,500 miles long? Name all the Canadian rivers that are less than 2,000 miles long but greater than 1,500 miles long.

Canada's Longest Rivers

River	Length (miles)
Mackenzie	~2,700
Yukon	~2,000
St. Lawrence	~1,900
Nelson	~1,600
Columbia	~1,250
Saskatchewan	~1,250
Peace	~1,200
Churchill	~1,000
South Saskatchewan	~850
Fraser	~850

Length (miles)

Making Waves

The world's largest indoor wave pool is in Canada—inside the world's largest shopping mall! West Edmonton Mall has an area of 5.3 million square feet. That is about the size of 92 American football fields! The mall also has an ice rink, an amusement park, a miniature golf course, an underwater submarine ride, and a life-size replica of Columbus's ship, the *Santa Maria*.

replica an exact copy

10

Figure It Out

How would you solve these wacky problems? (You may use a calculator to help.)

1. How many one-pint bottles of water would it take to fill the West Edmonton wave pool?

2. A household faucet delivers about 6 gallons of water per minute. Using one household faucet, would it take more or less than a year to fill the wave pool?

3. A bathtub holds about 40 gallons of water. How many bathtubs could be filled using the water in the wave pool?

Extra Challenge:

One gallon of water weighs 8.3 pounds. How many tons of water does the wave pool hold? (Hint: 1 ton = 2,000 pounds.)

Fun Facts

• The West Edmonton wave pool holds 2.7 million gallons of water.

• The water temperature is between 79°F and 86°F.

• There are 23 water slides. The tallest is 85 feet high.

• There are three whirlpools with a water temperature of 102°F.

Islands in the Ice

Canada has 52,455 islands. Some of these islands are very small. However, the largest, Baffin Island, is bigger than the state of California! Many of Canada's islands lie north of the mainland, close to Greenland and the Arctic Circle. These islands are surrounded by sea ice for much of the year.

Baffin Island

Some of Canada's most picturesque islands are in the St. Lawrence River. Although the area is called the Thousand Islands, the official count is 1,793 islands.

Canada has the world's largest lake on an island in a lake! Manitou Lake is located on Manitoulin Island, which is in Lake Huron.

Tremendous Tides

The biggest tides in the world occur on the east coast of Canada. Twice a day, more than three cubic miles of seawater rush into the Bay of Fundy and then pour out again. The water level at high tide can be as much as 52.5 feet higher than at low tide. That's higher than a five-story building!

Many of the cliffs around the Bay of Fundy have been worn away, or eroded, by the rushing seawater. In some places, all that remain of the cliffs are pillars with trees and plants on top. These stone pillars have been nicknamed "flowerpot rocks."

At the Bay of Fundy, high tides are approximately 12 hours and 25 minutes apart. (This time can vary by 15 minutes, depending on the wind, the position of the moon, and so on.)

Suppose that there is a high tide on Monday at 9 A.M. List the day and time for the next five high tides.

An Amazing Export

Canada produces more than four-fifths of the world's maple syrup. Each year, more than five million gallons of syrup are exported to the United States and other countries. Maple syrup is made by boiling down the sap from maple trees. This process was first used hundreds of years ago by Native North Americans.

Native Americans made maple syrup and maple sugar by putting heated stones into the sap to cook it. As the stones cooled, they were replaced by hot stones.

export   to send goods to another country for sale

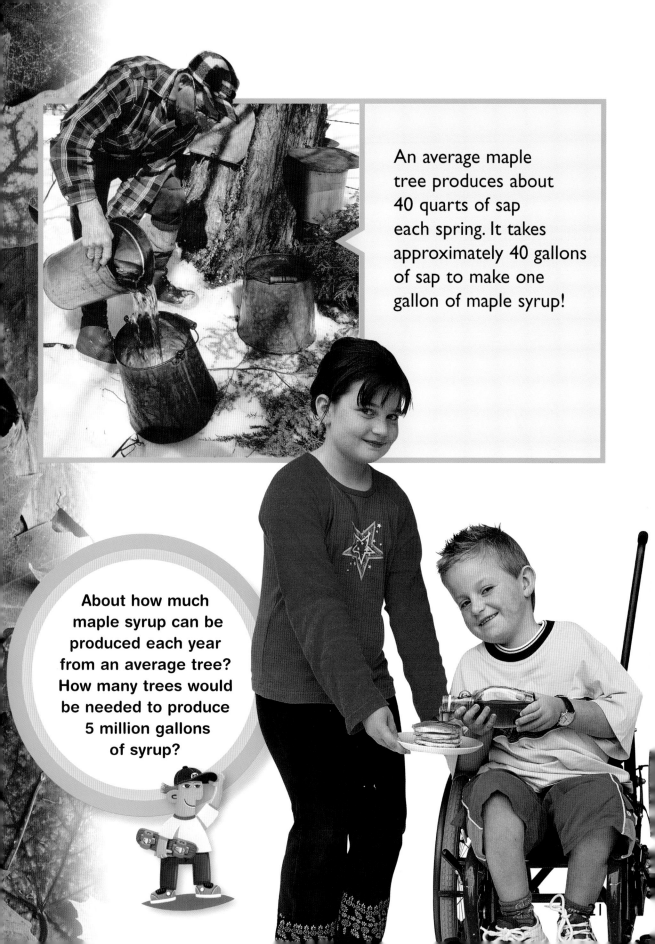

An average maple tree produces about 40 quarts of sap each spring. It takes approximately 40 gallons of sap to make one gallon of maple syrup!

About how much maple syrup can be produced each year from an average tree? How many trees would be needed to produce 5 million gallons of syrup?

Plotting the Population

When the first national census was taken in 1851, Canada had fewer than three million people. A century and a half later, the population was more than 30 million. If the countries of the world are listed in order of population, Canada ranks 34th out of 237. More than nine-tenths of Canadians live within 100 miles of the United States.

Canada's Population	
Census Year	Population (Millions)
1851	2.4
1861	3.2
1871	3.7
1881	4.3
1891	4.8
1901	5.4
1911	7.2
1921	8.8
1931	10.4
1941	11.5
1951	13.7
1961	18.2
1971	21.6
1981	24.8
1991	28.0
2001	31.0

Did You Know?

The red maple leaf flag became the national flag of Canada in 1965.

census   an official count of the number of people in a place

Make a Line Graph

To make a line graph that shows how Canada's population has grown, you will need a copy of the Blackline Master.

1. Find the population in 1851. (Use the chart on page 22.) Round it to the nearest million and show it on the graph.

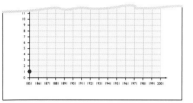

2. Round the 1861 population to the nearest million. Plot the next point.

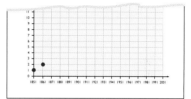

3. Keep going until you have plotted a point for each year on the chart.

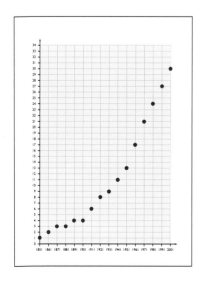

4. Draw lines to connect the points you plotted. (Use a ruler.) Add a title and labels to your graph.

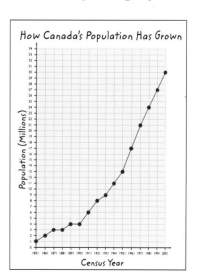

Sample Answers

Use the Internet to find out other interesting facts about Canada. For example, Canada has the longest national highway in the world. How long is the highway?

Page 4   2.74 million square miles

Page 7   1,435 lakes

Page 9   Nelson; St. Lawrence, Nelson

Page 11   1. 21.6 million bottles

           2. Less than a year (312.5 days)

           3. 67,500 bathtubs

           Extra Challenge: 11,205 tons

Page 15   Monday, 9:25 P.M.

           Tuesday, 9:50 A.M.; 10:15 P.M.

           Wednesday, 10:40 A.M.; 11:05 P.M.

Page 16   Heights in order (in feet) are:

           1,815; 1,762; 1,670; 1,535; 1,483;

           1,450; 1,427; 1,403; 1,381, 1,362

Page 19   Heights in order (in feet) are: 29,035; 22,841;

           20,320; 19,563; 18,481; 16,066; 7,310

Page 21   1 quart; 20 million trees

Index